Julia Coughs A Lot

Written By
Jo Oliver-Yeager, MS

Other Books By Jo Oliver-Yeager

Sophie Counts Her Steps
Adam (Sometimes) Can't Sit Still
Devon Missed the Joke
Sahith Read it Wrong

Copyright © 2021 Kind Words Publishing
ISBN 978-1-7358815-8-4

All rights reserved. This book may not be reproduced in whole or in part in any form, or by any means, without express written permission from the publisher.

Published by:
Kind Words Publishing
kindwordspublishing@gmail.com

Edited by:
Anthony Braca

This is dedicated to all the wonderful asthmatic people of the world.

This book is one in a series intended to educate people about acceptance and understanding as well as give a voice to anyone who may not fit into that "neat little box."

This story was inspired by my own personal experience. Thank you as well, to Julia Dunn who influenced the main character.

Embrace differences.

For my wonderful Tony and the inspiration of my three babies who hold my heart- Nyan, Tessa, & Auden for always supporting my love of writing.

Julia loves school as long as it means being inside. She especially likes lunchtime and library. But she is not a fan of gym class or recess. And she does not look forward to field trips.

Don't get her wrong, Julia likes the free time of recess or visiting new places. And don't most kids like recess because they can be free? Julia does enjoy that free time but only if it is warm outside (not too hot) and definitely not cold.

Julia does not enjoy those times as much as others because she is hiding something.

Julia had bronchitis the winter before.

Now she feels those symptoms at different times but she does not have bronchitis. Those symptoms get worse when it is too cold or too hot outside.

She also has an increase in symptoms during gym class when she runs too much. She was diagnosed with asthma.

She doesn't know anyone who has asthma besides herself.

She goes to the nurse's office when she has symptoms to use her inhaler. But she does *not* want to tell anyone.

Julia coughs a lot and people always ask her if she is sick. She would say no. But she knew coughing was sometimes part of having asthma.

She doesn't like that people move away from her when she is coughing. So she associates her symptoms with being treated like she is bad or has some catchy condition.

Julia wants to run outside with her friends in all weather. But she cannot.

She wants to go to ice skating parties or compete in sports at summer camp, but running makes her unable to breathe.

She is sometimes mocked for not being good at sports.

She is always chosen last for teams. Some friends don't even invite her to parties that involve physical activities. They figure she will not be able to take part.

She does not like being left out.

Julia noticed she was using her inhaler more than before. She reached out to her doctor.

They decided, along with Julia's parents, that she would start to take a preventative inhaler.

Julia saw the new inhaler as another thing to make her stand out. She already has the one to help when she can't breathe.

The doctor explained that the preventative medication will allow Julia to do more. He instructs Julia to take specific precautions.

She can warm up first before doing sports. She can wear a scarf or face mask during outdoor winter activities.

These habits will help warm up the air she is breathing. Then she will be able to go outside in winter with her friends.

For extreme heat, her doctor said most people cannot tolerate too much heat.

Julia should use her instincts and go to the shade or drink a lot of water. When possible, she should stay inside with air conditioning.

The next morning, she used her new preventative medication and went to school.

She realized she did not need to go to the nurse's office to use her fast-acting inhaler.

This gave her confidence that the preventative inhaler works.

She wanted to see if she could play with her friends outside. It was cold, but she wanted to try.

She put her scarf close around her neck and mouth and went out to play. She did not have an increase in symptoms. While she knew she wasn't cured, she felt more in control.

Her next big hurdle was being honest with her friends that she used an inhaler and had asthma.

At Lily's sleepover, Julia decided to tell her that she had asthma.

She pulled her inhaler from her backpack. She explained to Lily what it was for, and why she never liked gym or enjoyed playing outside sometimes.

Lily told Julia that her sister has asthma and uses the same inhaler.

Julia was feeling more confident. She also started to tell more people about her asthma.

It seems many people knew about inhalers. A few had used a nebulizer when they were sick.

Her friends and other classmates started being more understanding.

Julia still has moments when she has trouble breathing.

She is no longer afraid to use her inhaler in front of people, explain she has to "sit it out", or that she needs to go inside.

She started speaking up if she started to cough to say, "It's okay. I'm not sick. It's just my asthma."

Resources

- Asthma & Allergy Foundation of America
  https://www.aafa.org/

- Global Initiative for Asthma (GINA)
  https://ginasthma.org/

- Allergy & Asthma Network
  https://allergyasthmanetwork.org/

- World Allergy Organization
  https://www.worldallergy.org/

- American Academy of Allergy Asthma & Immunology (AAAI)
  https://www.aaaai.org/

- Global Allergy & Airway Patient Platform (GAAPP)
  https://gaapp.org/

www.ingramcontent.com/pod-product-compliance
Lightning Source LLC
Chambersburg PA
CBHW051305110526
44589CB00025B/2942